Dear Pamela

Dear Pamela
letters from a Radnorshire Farm

by
Taffy Prothero

Logaston Press

LOGASTON PRESS
Little Logaston Woonton Almeley
Herefordshire HR3 6QH

First published by Logaston Press 1997

ISBN 1 873827 10 5

Set in Times and Palatino by Logaston Press
and printed in Great Britain
by The Cromwell Press, Broughton Gifford

Acknowledgements

This book would never have seen the light of day unless friends and family of Taffy Prothero had transcribed the letters and checked the details with Taffy. In addition they have ferreted out the photographs and provided the information for the Introduction. In particular, thanks are given to Pamela Currie, the friend to whom the letters were addressed, Anne Ralphs, and to Richard Meredith and his family.

Introduction

Taffy was the name by which Miss Prothero most liked to be known, a constant reminder of her beloved Wales. In her later years she relived, with a deep and abiding satisfaction, the sights, sounds, incidents and people of her early years before The First World War on a farm in the parish of Llansantffraed-in-Elwel, an area more commonly known as Hundred House, a hamlet to the east of Builth Wellls.

Hundred House is a small, spread out settlement straddling the A481 Builth to Forest Inn road. Its centre, with its delights as described by Taffy, lies along the main road, but its population is and was then spread about the small farms in the valleys of the River Edw and its tributaries. But it is an old settlement. A tumulus lies south of the main road, and a Roman fort was built to the west of what is now the hamlet's centre and of which earthworks remain. Two border castles were also constructed. The first, Glan Edw, was probably commenced around 1093 by the English and is thought to have changed hands at least 5 times. It was succeeded by Colwyn Castle, built within the remains of the Roman fort. It too had a chequered border history.

Taffy was born in Adams Hill in Hereford, where her parents had been living for some time, on the 15th Febuary, 1901. She was the youngest of six—four girls and two boys—though the eldest boy had died in childhood before she was born. Her nearest sibling was a sister ten years her senior and for much of the time she grew up as if she was an only child.

Her letters relate to her time at Cwmberyn, a farm which lies below the hill of Carneddau near Hundred House. She believed that the farm 'had gone to an uncle and aunt and not my father, who was the elder brother, so he packed up and left.' But the family returned and her account portrayed hard working farmers where the basic needs were well provided for but frills neither available nor looked for. Taffy attended church and chapel each Sunday. In term time she walked to and from the school, a journey of some two and a half miles each way across country. Her clothes, long dresses and tight boots, she regarded as too restricting and she thoroughly approved of the relaxation in fashion which released young people into more casual clothes. Taffy was bright. She came top in the scholarship to grammar school, but her family considered such a move quite superfluous and Taffy never took up her place.

Taffy never married and her immediate family members have died. She was very attached to her niece, and great nephew and nieces all of who survive her.

In November 1917, Taffy joined the Women's Army Auxialiiary Corps, for much of the war working in the stores department in Nottingham. On discharge her character was recorded as having been 'excellent'. There can be no doubting that it was. Taffy always spoke of her army service years with great affection for she loved being busy and useful. It was there that she learned the skills of 'man management' which were to stand her in good stead during the library years which followed.

Leaving the Army in 1919, Taffy rode her motorbike to Norfolk taking up the task, together with her Commanding Officer from her Army days, Miss Newberry, of founding a county library. Its beginnings were humble enough: a large van full of books which Taffy drove from village to village. Stories abound of those embryo library years. One delivery to a Fenland village school involved putting the books in a box on a rowing boat propelled by the headteacher, Miss Denmark, who had been summonsed from the opposite river bank by the arrival of the van. The river route was necessary because the van was too heavy for the service road.

The project was a success. By the 1960s, Taffy had become County Librarian and presided over a fleet of vans and several branch libraries scattered throughout the county from an office at the heart of the purpose-built County Library headquarters in Norwich where, although in a different building, it is still to be found today. Taffy had done much to spread her love of literature and learning through the student service which she ran as part of the Library. To the suggestion that such was an achievement, Taffy would respond in her gentle, quiet voice 'oh no, no' and swiftly move to a new topic of conversation.

In retirement Taffy gave full reign to her reclusive tendencies. She loved her house and garden in Norwich and read keenly. She listened to the radio but never came to like or trust television—her natural intelligence was more than a match for its superficial inducements. Her main source of news was The Times in which she had done the crossword before most of us could have unfolded the paper. And, although to the casuual observer, out of touch, Taffy's insightful analysis of world affairs was always apposite.

Taffy's ready wit and quiet sense of hunour remained with her throughout her 95 years. Her long life gave time for falls and broken limbs. A broken wrist was followed by an arm then a femur. During a conversation with Taffy when she had moved to her last home, The Great Hospital, in Norwich, a friend remarked that she hoped that Taffy would not continue her quest for ever larger bones to break. Taffy replied 'I always was ambitious!'

The letters in this book are themselves a remarkable event. Two more disparate people than Taffy, reflective and retiring, and Pamela, colourful and ebullient, it would be hard to imagine. They met in Tisbury, Wiltshire, when Taffy was staying with a mutual friend. The spark was immediate. Pamela a catalyst to release Taffy's quietened tongue through correspondence. Sadly, Pamela's letters do not survive. For the most part they were designed to, and did, prime the pump to keep Taffy writing what soon became a fascinating autobiography for those who knew and loved her. Most of Taffy's letters are in this book where they speak for themselves.

Taffy died in July 1996.

7/10/84

Dear Pamela,

Thank you for your letter and news of my cardigan. I had never heard of a lined one before, but I think it is a very good idea, will slip on and off very easily. Yes, I think the brown, lemon and grey should wait for the present.

I have had a strong desire to record my early childhood days; a world that has completely vanished, and I am the only one left who knew my corner of it. It would be a pity for it to go completely. If you could share it with me I should feel content. The trouble is that it seems such a sensible thing to do when lying awake at nights, but take a pen in hand and the case is altered. It seems to grow unimaginably voluminous. Reminds me of the man who said 'Sorry this is such a long letter but I hadn't time to write a short one.' But my nonsense is not the sort of thing to condense. It was an age when we did not hurry, and consequently had plenty of time. The only thing to do is to try to pick off a morsel here and there; not that I have a lot to say, only a brief period of time.

Our parish concert should make a good start, for it was the one and only. Concerts in the Baptist Chapel in our parish and the Methodists in another were quite the ordinary thing, but one in our own little school room, and my Mother and Father went to it, that was news in itself because they always left such frivolities to my grown-up sisters and brother. I think it must have been in aid of some big parish or church project.

However, one dark, coldish night we set out to walk the mile and a half to the school; others lived a good deal further away. Arrived there, we found they had put trestle table tops over the desks in the infants' section, turned the other round at right angles, and hoisted a piano on to this platform. A paraffin lamp on the piano and another on the

1

table. And what a lovely, gentle light they gave, so different from the harsh white electric. Coming in from the dark, the stage looked almost brilliant compared with outside and with the 'auditorium' filled with people in dark clothes and lighted only by two one-candle power lamps fastened to brackets on the wall. Crowded, snug and warm.

I cannot remember anything about the Chairman, but the Squire opened the proceedings. He was a youngish man with already a fair-sized family, six or seven, they had a baby every year and it soon begins to add up. We clapped vigorously before and after every song. The one the Squire chose was:

> A simple youthful swain am I
> Who loves at fancy's pleasure.
> I fondly watch the blooming wheat
> While others reap the treasure.
> Oh, wherefore still despise my suit
> And pining keep thy lover
> For some new charm
> Than matchless fair
> I day by day discover.

I only wish I could provide you with the tune, I had a job to keep my pen from breaking out!

Next came our Schoolmaster with:-

> One Friday morn when we set sail,
> Our ship not far from land,
> We there did espy a fair, pretty maid
> With a comb and a glass in her hand.
> And the raging seas did roar
> And the stormy winds did blow
> And we jolly sailor boys
> Were all up aloft
> With the land lubbers lying down below,
> below, below.

At some point in this feast of song there came on my erstwhile rug mate. We might have just reached double figures, certainly not much more. He stuck his chest out manfully and delivered himself of:-

2

Oh, to reap and to sow
To plough and to mow
And to be a farmer's boy hoy hoy
And the last my memory holds - a young woman: -
Tis the last rose of summer
Left blooming alone
All her lovely companions
Are faded and gone.

How I would have loved to have sung all these songs and many more, but it was a no-go area for me. I couldn't sing anything in tune. In singing lessons with other children, the teacher would say 'Somebody is out of tune. You, stop.' I was talking about this to a clergyman in Norfolk who knew a lot about singing. He said 'But anyone who can hear, can sing.' I wonder if I had some slight congenital defect in my ear. But it was measles at twenty-five which put it out of action completely. A bit disappointing maybe, but how much worse never to have had the urge!

My handwriting has got very bad. A rather shaky hand but more from want of practice. 'Use it or lose it.' I realised I was writing little else than cheques, and they are not good practising material. So perhaps I have found the answer. To write small with a fine pen seems admirable; otherwise you might feel bludgeoned with a thick heavy one. With a fine pen one can creep up unawares, so to speak!

I think this must be all for today. I have other things to tell you, but they must wait for another time.

With my love, nostalgically yours,

Taffy

16/10/84

Dear Pamela,

As Radnorshire was a very thinly populated county, every-body was somebody; you couldn't afford to brush anybody off. But I remember particularly Mr and Mrs Sheen who were, I suppose, our chief family friends. They had known each other in Hereford, Mrs Sheen was around when I was born there. Why my parents were in Hereford it never occurred to me to enquire. I know they moved when an uncle of mine died young and left Father the farm; that was when I was six weeks old.

I never remember any mark of friendship between my Father and Mr Sheen, who were about as different as could be and rarely saw each other. Father would make some good-humoured scoffing remark about him occasionally. As for Mrs Sheen, Mother and I went to tea at Colwyn from time to time. She was very refined and the spitting image of Queen Alexandra. She had a daughter about my age called Violet whom I didn't care for much, at least not always.

Mr Sheen was interesting. One of those totally different types that a community will occasionally throw up. Over six foot tall, rather a haughty bearing, due probably to being a little short-sighted and in the habit of throwing his head back to see instead of peering forward. It was his mind though that was really remarkable. He could, and would, talk on any subject under the sun, at length. He would have matched Bernard Shaw or Bernard Levin for long involved sentences in which you felt he must lose his way; but, no, he riveted all together in the end perfectly. I could have listened to him for ever. Poor Man! He was born before his time. What a shine he would have made on our media! I remember only one remark of his. Somebody asked him what he thought of our vicar's sermons. 'Sermons!!!', he said, 'Why, I could write better sermons, get them printed, and sell them for a farthing a yard.'

And then there was Charley Price, our roadman, who seemed to be inseparable from a heap of stones and a sledge hammer. Cart-loads full were tipped by the side of the road at intervals, and it was Charley's job to break them up small enough for the steam roller to crush them, which it did, like pats of butter. Nobody, child or adult, would pass Charley without stopping to talk. He and I had the Crippen murder case over from every conceivable angle.

He was in the habit of chewing twist. I don't suppose you have heard of it? It looked like black sticks of liquorice all-sorts, but it was dark brown and made of tobacco. You cut off a piece about half-an-inch long, popped it in your mouth and chewed. This demanded, as you can imagine, frequent expectoration, which Charley accomplished with admirable expertise. But I was never sure whether this compensated for the practice.

Poor Charley was really poor. When he had chewed and assuaged his longing, he would take the piece out of his mouth and put it in his waistcoat pocket, saving it to be brought out later when the yearning returned. People did say that when he ran out of pence, he cut his waistcoat pockets out and chewed them.

Talking of 'coats' reminds me of a story about our Vicar seeing Charley in a new coat. 'You are very smart, Charley, where did you get your new coat from?' 'Same place as you, sir, the Parish.'

But to return to Mr Sheen, who at this particular time had just had his seventieth birthday and, being a County Councillor and JP and very well known local figure, had been noticed in the local paper and properly buttered up. During the same week or ten days several local men just turned seventy had died, perhaps as many as four or five. It was the talking point just then; who would be next? Now Charley detested Mr Sheen. One morning just then Mr Sheen was walking along the road and Charley was there with his heap of stones:-

'Morning, Charley!'

'Morning, Mr Sheen, big call for men of your age just now.'

18/10/84

Dear Pamela,

For a short time, perhaps a month or six weeks, we had our very own parochial Private Eye; anonymous, in verse, manuscript, gratis and post free.

I remember when this rather bulky envelope arrived and the taking out of the lined foolscap content. We could hardly believe our eyes, all the gossip that nearly everybody knew but would be very chary of expressing; put here straight from the shoulder, sharp and tart. Who was the author? We hadn't a clue. Why had we been favoured with it? But when we got out and about we found everybody else had had it too, by the same post.

Unfortunately I can remember only a fragment of the family long 'poem'. A bachelor who had fallen ill had been taken in and cared for by a family to whom he left in his Will some small amounts of money. Private Eye felt it should all have gone to his sister Anne. Other people had been attentive in visiting him. PE wrote about our Mr Sheen:-
'Made himself a sudden friend/And kept it up until the end.' (It's a lie, said Mr Sheen, we were boys together.) But it was the caring family that PE really had it in for:-
   The Missus fifty quid like oil.
   The daughter must an heiress be
   For fifty quid I hear has she.
   The sons a ten pound note apiece,
   But they must not the whole lot fleece,
   For someone says that if they can
   They must leave fifty quid for Anne.

The parish was in a ferment. I'll find out who he is, I'll take him to court, etc. etc. But they never did.

The second one arrived about a month later. I can remember only the first verse of this, which was about a widower marrying his housekeeper. Now Radnorshire people hated any showing off, ostentation, drawing attention to oneself. There was an undrawn Plimsoll line, and you must not go above it. Young people getting married could throw their heels up a bit, but not too much. But a widower and his housekeeper, this was a case clearly calling for something quiet and unobtrusive. But what did the man go and do but hire a motor car from Llandrindod, the only one in the place. It was the talking point and joke all around.

PE started off this effusion with:-

> It is a secondhanded marriage
> My friends I write about,
> It happened on a Wednesday
> When the motor car was out.

PE must have made between twenty and thirty copies, all in imitation copperplate, for, of course, he couldn't use his own handwriting. This is quite a lot of work. But the fun of waking up on the great morning, knowing you had set everyone by the ears!

It needed organising too. A farmer with a strong taste for foolscap paper would stand out in Builth. He must have got his wife to get it in Llandrindod in the season when the visitors were there.

19/10/84

Dear Pamela,

Llandrindod Wells cannot be passed without comment.
Minus the 'Wells' there seems to be no reason why it should
have been anything other than a typical local parish. It had
no particular advantage such as the Wye at Builth nor had it
ever had a market. It had a lake certainly which was pleasant
to look at, but no local person would have dreamt of taking a
boat and rowing on it.

No, the reason for Llandrindod becoming a small town
was that in the latter part of the nineteenth century the
medical profession embraced the belief that the cure for
most human ills was to drink water from certain springs
with medicinal values; the smellier the better! Llandrindod
had four or five. I only remember Chalybeate. People had to
come to the place to 'take the waters', and stay for a few
weeks. So, hotels and boarding houses sprang up in an
incredibly short time to cash in on this opportunity. Farmers'
surplus daughters saw their chance and went in to run them.
Llandrindod waxed exceedingly.

Its heyday was in my time, particularly in the First World
War when the Upper Crust came because they couldn't go
abroad. 'Trains up and down, six hours from Euston, twice
daily.' Everything was done to attract them, everywhere was
painted up spick and span; croquet lawns and bowling
greens in the centre were mown, edges trimmed,
blue-chipped gravel paths raked, and flowers in profusion.
Tennis and golf links nearby. And in the lovely summer
evenings pierrots in The Rock Park. Landaus waiting to take
you for a country drive in the afternoon.

The shop assistants' half-day holiday was packed up by
general consent in the season; who could think of shops
being shut so many people around with money to spend!

Grocers' shops were open on Saturdays—incredibly—from 7.30 a.m. to 10.30 p.m.

There was a Ladies Choir, two or three hundred strong, all in white, flanked by a couple of large harps on either side. They sang before Edward VIIth at the opening of the Rhayader Water Works to supply Birmingham. They sang, of course, 'Land of Hope and Glory'.

We took a great personal interest and pleasure in our distinguished visitors. The Brecon & Radnor published a comprehensive list each week, and in strict order of precedence of place and person, beginning with 'The Pump House Hotel, the Marchioness of Carisbroke' and down through the whole gamut ending with 'Myrtle Villa, the Misses Price of Bargoed.'

How nostalgic to think of the horse-drawn vehicles belonging to the various hotels with drivers in uniform, top hats, and epaulets on their shoulders with fringes, and the boots, all little buttons down the front, and a round pill box hat on their heads!

I wish I could draw and sketch. When I used to walk to Landrindod in the holidays I sometimes saw on the hill on my left, fairly high up, the figure of a horsewoman all in black, not young; one of the sisters who invited me to tea later on, riding her pony round the corner of the hill, silhouetted against the sky. Side saddle of course, with a pannier strapped on one side of the pony and a big basket on her left arm; taking eggs and butter to sell in Llandrindod, the very last to do so. The old world was expiring bit by bit.

21/10/84

Dear Pamela,

What games and amusements were there for everybody; children and adults. Well, the adults didn't expect any. There was market day once a week when you met people and talked, and the men went into pubs but not the women. And there was Church and Chapel on Sunday.

The children had the usual games; rounders, tick, blind man's buff, etc, and knew all the necessary rhymes—not from any book, but handed down. The boys played football, which I liked and was allowed to play quite often because there were not enough boys to make up two sides. The girls had a cissy game called 'House'. Some large stones, of which there were plenty around, were arranged and imagined into chairs and couches in a fine drawing room, and bits of broken china into an elegant tea service. And elegant we certainly had to be. These 'cups' were not taken hold of anyhow, they had to be held between thumb and forefinger, and the rest of the fingers fluted out fanwise, particularly the little finger. There was nearly a fight amongst the others as to who should be hostess. And who do you suppose the hostess was? None other than Lady Diana Manners!

It still puzzles me how news of this lovely and lively young lady percolated through to our quiet corner. Not through the Brecon & Radnor, nor Answers or Titbits or the Daily Mail! Perhaps London Opinion was in print then. If so, it would certainly be on the bookstalls in Llan'dod.

Somebody over sixty years of age asked me the other day 'Who was Lady Diana Manners?' Brought up in Norwich too.

On the afternoon of the last Friday in July we had a breaking-up school tea party. Lessons in the morning as usual, but all of us in our best clothes and quietly seething with anticipation. Games and mild competitions in the afternoon; then the tea, with plenty of everything usually available only sparingly if at all and 'not good for you'. And to wind up, 'Kiss in the ring', which we did not play at any other time.

But the gala days were the two May Fairs, a fortnight in between, on a parkland beside the Wye. When you went in there was a big steam engine providing heat for cooking chipped potatoes. They smelt delicious. I wanted some, never having had one in my life, but my parents said 'Certainly not. They cook them in cart-wheel grease.'

There was all the familiar stalls and amusements. My father spotted a tent advertising 'Moving pictures'. We went in and stood on a wooden platform five feet or so high. The tent was dark but we could just see the green grass between us and the other end where there was a big white screen. Presently the show began, figures moved on the screen jerkily and it appeared to be raining heavily. But we could follow what was going on. That evening at home my father said 'I think there is a great future for these moving pictures.' 'Surely not,' said Mother, 'people would never waste their money on such nonsense.' Father was right that time.

27/10/84

Dear Pamela,

The slightest attempt to recall Edwardian Radnorshire would be lop-sided without mention of our ghosts, for they were nearly as numerous and almost as well known as the fleshly inhabitants. There were spine-chilling stories in plenty and places well known to be their favourite haunts.

In our family we did not talk about them, so I must have picked up the stories from outside. Strangely, I have forgotten them all except one absurdity:- a waggoner had taken his gambo to the mill with sacks of grain to be ground. He had stopped to talk as usual and it was dark when he set off for home. He had just started to get up the Disserth pitch when the horses suddenly went berserk, tried to gallop uphill and came out all of a lather. He was almost tossed about trying to hold them in, and happening to glance at the back of the gambo he saw two silent figures in cloaks, and cowls on their heads. He could do nothing about it as he tugged at the reins to keep on the road. Relating this horrific experience in the local pub next evening he said 'And they didn't disappear until we were right in the fold at Cwmbach.' 'Caught sight of the Missus?' suggested one bright spark. Point well taken, for the Missus was well known to be a forceful dame.

Incidentally, a gambo is a kind of light, open dray used for carting hay; entirely forgotten now. A pitch is what the English call a hill. We had so many real hills around that we were forced to find another word for a steep road.

But we didn't joke about ghosts as a rule, very far from it. Schoolgirls would have a serious consultation as to what was best to do if we were to meet with one. A girl who seemed to know a lot about it said 'You must never say anything to them. Instead, make the sign of the Cross on your breast and say "In the name of ..."' This seemed to me to

13

be quite sound, but what if you cried out in alarm? 'Ah, then you would put yourself in their power.' It seemed to me to be very difficult.

And not only were the girls overawed by them, but the boys too. One young man lost his life through it. Several of them had walked together to Builth on a Saturday night and intended to come back together as usual, but one of them missed linking up with the rest—stayed too long with his girl friend I expect. This poor young man dare not walk alone in the dark by the notoriously haunted White Bridge, so he hung about till daybreak. A cold, long night, he caught a chill, it turned to pneumonia and he died.

Now, the ghosts have gone with the wind, entirely a thing of the past. A lot of moonshine, people say. Certainly a very large part of it was, but I think the changed circumstances should be considered. To see a ghost one needed to be on foot or on horseback. Now nobody goes on foot or horseback after dark. They all go in cars. What chance does a ghost stand of being seen in the headlights of a fast-moving car? I wonder how they feel about it.

A rather strange experience fell to the lot of my father and eldest sister. They had been to Shrewsbury Flower Show in the middle of August, a favourite outing locally. They travelled back to Llan'dod on the last train with a lot of friends and had a very pleasant time. They also had company for the first five or six miles of the walk home, until they branched off to take a short cut across country. It was a light night and mild. They got to the next farm to ours, Cefnbuchan, through the fold and out on to Cefnbuchan Bank which was open and from which you could see our house, with a little white square of a lighted window. Somebody waiting up, of course. They were quite relaxed, almost at home. Father saw that Mr Bowen had moved his cattle into an adjoining field to ours and said he hoped they wouldn't break through this time.

And then their attention was riveted. A woman all in black had come in at the other end of the lane. Who on earth could she be? A woman out alone after midnight? Too tall

14

for so-and-so, not the right walk for another. Something must be very wrong somewhere. She came on to meet them and when she was near enough my Father moved his tongue to say 'Good night. Are you in trouble? Can we help?' When—she vanished.

I have no theory about this. I just don't know.

2/11/84

Dear Pamela,

Radnorshire is very beautiful by night, in shiny moonlight or, which I think I prefer, with a 'matt finish' of soft French grey, as light almost as day in high summer.

In daytime too. I remember one March morning when I had to walk to Llandrindod very early when everywhere was stiff with hoar frost under a reddish mackerel sky. All as pure and fresh as on the first day of creation. Every footstep a crunch. When I got to the top of the valley and had a wide view I saw the smoke beginning to rise straight up from farmhouse chimneys.

In late June or early July it was the scent of the new-mown hay, the little lanes festooned with pink and white dog-roses, and children searching the ditch sides for wild strawberries.

August too had its speciality. Sometimes when I was home on holiday and would wake up early, have a look out of the window and realise that it was going to be a very hot day, I would see the mist starting to creep up the valley— white as milk; well, poorish skim milk faintly tinged with blue, but diaphanous. It would come on at what seemed a walking pace—you could hardly believe it. Gradually it would fill up everywhere; fields, woods, buildings would be lost, only the hill tops remaining. When the sun grew strong, all would soon disappear.

Radnorshire is a poor county, only between 17,000 and 18,000 inhabitants seven years ago, and not a traffic light in the place.

A long time ago somebody wrote a rhyme:-
Radnorshire, poor Radnorshire,
With never a park and never a deer
Never a squire with more than five hundred a year
Excepting for Richard Fowler of Abbey-cwm-hir.

And now they have taken the very name away. We form a part of Powys.

'Cursed be he who removeth his neighbour's landmark.'

But it still keeps its hold on us. I know a native, not yet fifty years of age, who calls to see me sometimes just to run his tongue over the old names. As homesick as a dog, he is. His wife, who has a plum job here, would exchange it for something less in Mid-Wales to give him his heart's desire. I am not sure I want it to come off—it's 'such stuff as dreams are made of.'

To continue our parish annals, I have to strike a sad and tragic note. Our Squire met with a sudden and untimely end. They had been felling trees and were clearing the timber away, a rough and hard job with cart horses and iron chains over uneven ground, a piece swung out at an angle, they couldn't hold it and it hit the Squire on the head and killed him. The parish was very deeply shocked—dumbfounded. It was decided that we should build a church hall as a memorial, which was done, and it stands to this day—The James Vaughan Memorial Church Hall.

Young Jim carried on for a few years with his mother, but he couldn't play his father's part, and times were against him! 'End of an era' for so many things. He sold his farms at the bottom of the market in the post-war slump, married and moved away.

We sold our farm too for next to nothing, despite Mother's opposition. She was the one with the commonsense, but wasn't listened to. My brother was either the sixth or the seventh generation, and here is a little housekeeping observation—there was the same floor covering throughout, and still is as far as I know. It is now somebody's holiday retreat. The ground floor had a stone floor throughout, blue-ish grey tiles, flagstones (or slabs) about a yard square. When they needed cleaning, you washed them, simple as that! The bedrooms had oak floors boards, about 10" or a foot wide.

Imagine yourself as a small child coming downstairs to those stone floors on a cold winter's morning, the house feeling like a church, for all the windows were covered with

'Jack Frost's flowers'. You couldn't see out at all—stained glass windows, but all in an austere white-ish grey, and the shapes as varied and beautiful as any flowers of the field or garden. (Central heating and Jack Frost's flowers cannot get on together; sheer incompatibility).

When the fire in the big grate (perhaps on humanitarian grounds I ought to have mentioned before that there was a fire!) had been going for some time and a lot of hot tea had been made and consumed, the windows began to show signs of thawing, very small and only one at first. Somebody would lift me up, take me to this small hole and say 'Let's look at the cows being let out.' And out they came slowly one by one. White-faced Herefords, but against the deep snow almost yellow-faced, their breath in trumpets of vapour into the frosty air. They slowly made their way to the brook at the side of our fold, a black cut between deep snowy sides, and took their morning drink. How cold it must have been, but they didn't seem to mind.

Later, when the flowers were really beginning to thaw, I was lifted up to watch the horses. This, for me, was the great event of the day for they rolled in the snow, their hides no doubt itchy from the hay seeds filtered down from the loft over the stable. The carters were splendid with their great hoofs in the air, they rolled right over and I cheered with all my might.

We were un-moneyed people as nearly everybody was in those days, and we were likely to remain so. Oh, we were careful enough with the small change—compulsory subject, but we let the main chances go by, some in rather odd ways! A tenant farmer determined to buy his farm, the bargaining long and hard, but at last when it was settled, Tom Price saddled his pony, took a smallish hessian bag in his hand, rode in to Builth to the solicitors and paid the price in gold sovereigns which had then appreciated in value very considerably.

A rather odd local chap had a mind to buy a small holding; when at last the sale was agreed, he and the vendor decided to hand over the money at the local shop and post office and get Mr Williams to check it for them as he was more used to handling money. This he willingly agreed to do, but he rather repented of it, for the purchaser brought the money in a tin box, all in 10/- notes and all folded up nearly as small as postage stamps. 'But, Billy, why in 10/- notes?' 'Ah,' said Billy, with the smug satisfaction of being one step ahead, 'I heard the pound was losing its value, so I changed all of mine.'

And not only with money. Also with time. Towards the end of the 1914-18 War when I was home for a few days holiday, two elderly spinster sisters invited me to tea at four o'clock. When I arrived I noticed that the grandfather clock said five past three. 'Oh, you haven't moved your clock on!' 'Oh, no,' they replied, 'we must keep one at the old time. It would be a terrible thing if we lost the real time.'

2/11/84

Dear Pamela,

Time has moved on; we have moved from peace into war, and I from childhood to adolescence. The postman came and said he had just delivered calling-up papers on two men who we all felt certain would be exempt for they were so clearly unsuitable for military service. It was not a re-assuring sign.

Things were not going well. I said to Mother 'I want a serious talk with you. We have just heard what sort of straits they are in to call up Y and Z. There is only one thing for it—they will have to take women for the Army. What else can they do? It will surely come. And when it does you realise that I shall have to go? I am not raising a family nor working in munitions, so I am just what they will be looking for. Could we talk this over now and get it settled so that at the time there need be no fuss, as there was when Jack went. (Father had turned him out.) We don't want to make an exhibition of ourselves. You do understand, don't you?' 'Oh yes,' Mother said, 'no doubt you will carry your rifle as well as the rest of them, and you have always wanted to wear trousers.' I didn't care for the sound of the rifle very much, and as for the trousers, what sensible woman on a farm would wear anything else. They all do now.

I seemed to have got this question settled much more easily than I should. Perhaps Mother did move with the times more quickly than I had given her credit for, though I did think she had given me rather a short answer.

Some time during that summer a married sister who was living near Harrogate came home with her two small boys for a few days holiday. She was my youngest sister, about ten years older than me. I had three sisters, all more like aunts than sisters to me, and aunts I didn't see very much of as they were away in jobs or married and only home for brief spells. There couldn't be any companionship because the age gap was too wide and the contacts too brief. Also I was an entirely mother-centred child.

This youngest sister had been a very nice looking girl—the local beauty in fact. English rose complexion, good features, deep blue eyes and hair the colour of a ripe cornfield with just a glint of auburn. She had young men galore, and liked them. They sent her postcards thick and fast, often of lovely young actresses like Phyllis and Zena Dare and Marie Studholme, etc, which seemed to me to be rather a curious way to express their devotion. But it seemed to go down all right.

Two brothers had a regular set to about her. Both wanted her, but both couldn't go courting, it would have been absurd, so they had to settle which it was to be. They started to argue about it after they went to bed one night, the argument got very hot, nothing to do but to get out and fight. They fought with such vim that one knocked the other clear through the partition into the room where their parents were sleeping! A disturbed night all round at Bryncrath! I don't suppose that the partition was very substantial, probably lath and plaster, but even so it was roughish.

My sister was not in the least spoilt by all this attention. She hadn't a vestige of that in her nature, and now with housekeeping cares and children I expect she had forgotten all about it.

While she was at home the idea came about that I might go back with her and lend her a hand. Oddly, I cannot remember how I received this. Adolescents are sometimes casual and vague beyond belief. Could this have been the case? Anyway, I went.

My brother-in-law had been managing Ogden's jewellry and fine arts shop in Llan'dod, a branch of their Harrogate business. He was friendly with the young Ogdens. That seemed to be the right setting for this faultlessly tailored and carefully manicured young man, but what must he go and do but take a strong fancy to a farmer's life! We held up our hands in horror, but it was no good. He got a farm near Starbeck, three or four miles out of Harrogate and about a quarter of a mile along the lane from his parents' house. This

The Farm

Hundred House Inn, as drawn in 1983

Taffy's father

Taffy's mother and sister Lizzie

Taffy Prothero

Builth Wells High Street

was about two or three years before war broke out. And that was to be my home for the immediate future.

I didn't take to it particularly well. Fruitless now to go into detailed reasons. Obviously it was a big change. The in-laws, the Chippindales were quite all right to me, but they were strangers in my eyes. My sister had to warn me—prepare me I should say—that when Mr Chippindale called, it was his invariable custom to kiss every woman member of the family both on arrival and departure, and that I wasn't to mind. I got quite used to these encounters with a limp scrubbing brush, but I thought it very odd.

They were rigid teetotallers. When one of the two daughters was desperately ill, the doctors ordered brandy to restore her, but her father said 'No'. She pulled through. That was very different from our side; my Father said to me one day 'Always keep a drop of brandy in the house. Never have anything to do with a cheap brandy, it's no use to you. You can't go wrong with Martell's Three Star.' That was all the advice he ever gave me. (He was no tippler, by the way.)

They also regarded smoking by women as unspeakably obnoxious. I loved my cigarettes, but I couldn't smoke in the open. My sister liked one very occasionally, but she always wore gloves to smoke in order to be sure the scent wasn't obvious. Pitiful! Why can't people be content to live blameless lives themselves and trust that the example will be irresistible to others?

Mrs Chippindale was one of the nicest people you could meet, but I never got to know her. I don't see how I could.

Time went on and I got more and more a fish out of water, but I kept it absolutely to myself. My sister and brother-in-law did not seem to enjoy life very much. She was over anxious and rather a perfectionist and he suffered from devastating headaches. And, looking back over nearly seventy years, I don't suppose I was exactly a little ray of sunshine, however hidden my discontent may have been. Some housework and pushing the pram out were not enough. I wanted something to get my teeth into.

I didn't like my sister's friends, particularly her chief one who lived along the lane and was rather a trend setter. I remember our going to tea there one cold wet afternoon. A nice house but I didn't like the room where we had tea. There was a very black Jacobean dresser which looked as if the stain had been brushed on to bare wood; no sanding, no polish. A fashion just then I believe. It held a tea service in a very harsh blue with a heavy floral design. And we had funny bright yellow little cakes to eat. I formed the opinion they were made of Indian meal which we fed the hens on at home. The taste bore it out.

Coming back from there, I thought 'Oh, if only I could get out of all things.' And that became the background of my mind. I even thought of suicide, not resolutely nor in detail, but just as a solution. If only I could 'fade upon the midnight air' as Keats had said. I wonder if this is all that unusual in teenagers? And if it explains their taking to drugs. If so, they have my sympathy. I saw my life stretch out like a bleak, monotonous, arterial road, notched up, not with milestones, but with decades; sixteen now, twenty-six, thirty-six, forty-six, why people even lived to be sixty-six! Oh, take it away!

In the same predicament, I should feel the same today.

The bright spots were when I was sent up to Harrogate to do a little family shopping. I didn't have to hurry back. I could spend an hour or two looking at the shops and mooching around, which I enjoyed. I am a born loner. And in family life there is not much privacy. There was plenty at home; in the lumber room, the farm buildings, the fields, and, of course, the long walks which were part of our daily lives, or, at least, of mine.

On this particular afternoon just as I had done all on my list, it came on to rain, cold and heavy. I was disgusted. Nothing to do but get an early bus back. As I was walking along I saw an open door and on the hall table a small framed notice 'Madame Rita, Clairvoyant'. By Jove, I thought, the very thing. I will go in and pay somebody to talk to me, engage them, employ them. The waiting room was on the first floor, so up I went.

I was a bit nervous. Clairvoyants were gypsies, weren't they? Yellow skin, black coils of oily hair, scrawny hands. Would I manage not to squirm when she took hold of mine to read my palm? A nice little waiting room, but nobody about. I turned my attention to the papers. Well, gypsy or no gypsy, she keeps a good table of magazines, I thought. They were all there—Punch, the Field, the Lady, the Tatler, the Sphere, etc, etc.

I took up the Tatler which had quite large pages, not very many but fine art paper, very good for photographs. And photographs there were, every week, a couple of pages, passport size, of handsome young men, a caption under each telling of public school, university, military or naval establishment, regiment, ship, a detail of service perhaps, but the concluding line the same for all:- 'Killed in action.' I thought it was sad. But I started to look at them to see which was the most attractive. It wasn't easy. They all appealed to me in their very different ways. I got absorbed in this and failed to notice that someone had come into the room until there was a slight cough.

I looked up, and had the biggest surprise of my life:- no gypsy, but a nice looking lady in full evening dress. I had never before seen anyone togged up to this extent. Speechless admiration on my part.

'You wanted to see me?' she said.

'Yes, please.'

'Well, I am going to the opera later this evening. We are going out first. Some friends are coming for me in half-an-hour. I can give you twenty minutes, if that will do.'

'Yes, please.'

She took me into her room, and what a pleasant room it was, gave me a chair and looked at my hand. 'A very good life line. You will live on into old age.' (So bemused, entranced was I that I forgot this was precisely what I did not want!) She went on to talk about 'auras'; said I had a very good one. That is, I had a nice disposition. Very nice hearing. She said 'You are not happy where you are. I wonder why.' I took this to be just a statement, and not a leading question. So we passed on. The interview came to an end.

It was all over, and I realised my 'road' was waiting for me outside. It was a very bad moment. I thought I had better get out quick! But she detained me, 'No hurry. When you are up in Harrogate and if you have time, and if you would like to, call in and see me. Not to consult me, of course, but just for a chat. If I am with a client, of course, I cannot see you, but if I am free, I shall be pleased. I would like to know how you go on.' My spirits took a flying leap from zero to zenith!

I told them about it when I got back to the Farm. 'What did she tell you? Can you remember it all?' etc. But when I said I was going to see her again, my sister said 'But that's absurd. You can't have more than one future. You certainly don't need to go again.' How thankful I should be that my sister was an essentially gentle person, not a coarse-grained clodhopper who would have said 'You are not to go and see her again. D'you hear what I tell you?' No, but she wasn't happy about it.

However, not long after when I was in Harrogate Rita said 'You know, if your sister would care to come and see me she would be very welcome. Perhaps you will mention it to her and if she agrees, suggest a date.' This was done without delay, but the meeting was not a terrific success, no rapport. The next time we met, Rita said 'You know, you were born older than your sister is now.' It was the only strange remark she ever made to me. I can't say that I understood it. I felt that there was still a background of disapproval, and not only or mainly at the Farm.

Now, Mrs Chippindale was good enough to let us have her charwoman one day a week, washing day. I sometimes had to take messages to her in her little house in Starbeck. I soon got to know her well enough to say when I arrived 'Let's send out for some fish and chips' and Mrs Foster would go, and we would have a nice little feast. This had to be very sub rosa.

A little while later on, Mrs Foster and I were alone in the kitchen of the Farm when she said 'They were talking about you at Mrs Chippindale's the other day, Miss.'

'Oh, whatever did they find to say about me?'

'Well, it was Miss Meggie. I was clearing the table. Mr Amos was sitting in an armchair looking at the paper (Mr Amos was the head of the family and most highly regarded) and nearly snoozing I believe, when Miss Meggie said "I wonder that Mrs Chippindale doesn't put her foot down about that young sister of hers going up to Harrogate to consult a clairvoyant. Madame Rita I think she calls herself." Mr Amos stirred himself and said "Eh, Meggie, what did you say? Did I hear you say 'Rita'. Why, she couldn't do better. She is one of the nicest women in Harrogate. I go to see her myself from time to time.""

I did whenever I had a chance, always taking a nice bunch of flowers from the nearby florist as an expression of my regard.

One evening Rita said 'I think we might try the crystal. We haven't done so, so far, have we?' She got out the ball of clear glass about the size of a golf ball and told me to hold it in both my hands for a few seconds. She took it and said 'Oh, a very clear picture. Definitely there is a move in store for you and soon. Six! Six weeks, that's very soon. Six months, that's too long. I can see a room, a big room, with a lot of people in it, crowded in fact. And what is very puzzling is that they are all dressed alike. Why? It is a well lighted room, and cheerful. Probably an open fire. But what I cannot make out is that there is a haze, almost a fog, over all. Now, how can that be in a brilliantly lighted room? The picture is clear, but I cannot interpret it.'

I didn't take very much notice of this. When I was there I liked to shut out the world as far as possible and to forget it. It all seemed very remote.

Time went on, and life in the usual way. One day I had to go up and back as quickly as possible to get something that was wanted at once. Walking down the main street I saw a shop that had been empty was taken. I glanced to see what sort of a business it was, and there was only a big poster of women in khaki greatcoats with haversacks on their backs 'Women's Army Auxiliary Corps wants <u>YOU</u>.'

I went in and got particulars including an application form, and took it back. Very sub rosa, of course. Looking at it in my bedroom I read that the minimum age for joining was eighteen. This was early November, and I wouldn't be seventeen until next February. Well, I thought, if I put eighteen, they will think 'Is she really eighteen!' So I put nineteen, feeling that nobody would think anyone would be silly enough as to stick on another year.

The next time I saw Rita, I showed her all this. She tested me very thoroughly about Mother having agreed when I spoke of the possibility. She knew I was telling the truth (as I knew it), but she couldn't understand it. However, I made it quite clear that I was going to press on. She said 'Well, if you are sure, you had better find the best way of doing it. I know a colonel who could advise you. I will get in touch with him.'

So she did, and I had to go to a big house on the Ripon Road, and was shown into the dining room. The colonel sat at one end of the long table and I at the other, and it would have been hard to say which was the more ill at ease. We didn't make much progress. Then he had a bright idea. 'I will send for my sergeant. He knows all these details better than I do.' So in came the sergeant, all smart and alert. 'So you want to join the Army, Miss, do you? What as?'

'Oh, anything to get in.'

'You mustn't talk like that. You want to consider, look around, and see what is best. Would you like to be a cook?'

'No, I couldn't do it.'

'A kitchen Maid?'

'Er, well—to get in.'

The sergeant made a gesture of impatience:-

'A storewoman?'

'Oh yes, much better.'

'A clerk?'

'Yes, best of all. I think I could do it. I have had a little experience.'

'There, you see, you need to look around!'

So 'Clerk' went in on my application form, which I sent off without delay.

I didn't say anything to anybody. They may well send my form back with 'Be your age' or some such written across it. Time enough when I heard from them.

And I did hear from them—calling me up before the Medical and Selection Boards at Doncaster. Now the fat was properly in the fire. Mother had completely forgotten our conversation, and everybody was against me. However, I would not be deterred. (To have lived through this patch once is enough. I will not elaborate.)

I had never put my hair up, a lot of it, very curly and short. No good going with my hair down in those days, so I bought a packet of hairpins, and on the morning of the fateful day stuck them all into my defenceless head, and managed to ram a hat on top. I looked quite nineteen I should think!

I got through the medical without difficulty and was ushered into Selection. The officer (all women officers of course) said to me after brief preliminaries 'What glass would you serve such-and-such a wine in?' I had never heard of the wine, let alone the glass. She asked me one or two more such questions with equally blank results. Oh dear, I thought, they want experienced women of the world who are used to dining and wining. I shouldn't have thought it necessary. Fancy my thinking that a country simpleton like me would be what they are looking for.

The prospect of slinking back with my tail between my legs began to face me. I expect I went very white. The officer looked worried, and started to say 'I wonder why ...' when the N.C.O. hurried in: 'Very sorry, ma'am, you have been given the wrong papers, should have been for a clerk and not a wine waitress!'

After that we got on much better, and soon she was saying 'Well, we are willing to take you, but think carefully; are you sure you still want to join? You are quite free to change your mind now, no penalty. But if you sign this form you sign your freedom away for the duration. You will be sent here or there, recalled, given work to do, have it taken away, etc. You will belong to the Army and not to yourself.' I said 'I do want to join.' I could hardly wait to get hold of that pen!

I sallied forth into the street. It was lunch time. The N.C.O. and two or three friends were walking a little ahead of me. She turned and said over her shoulder 'If you want a place for lunch, so-and-so's down the road isn't bad.' 'Thank you'

I said. These splendid women recognize me as one of themselves! I glowed with pride and pleasure.

Mercifully, the period between Doncaster and call-up was brief. My papers and railway warrant came, and next morning I set off with suitcase in hand, black velour hat on head, and wearing a grey woollen coat, and with not a care in the world. The world was my oyster! Such is youth. There is nothing like it. I am very thankful to have had a taste.

My destination was the Arboretum in Nottingham. This was a big glass pavilion in their central park, used for summer entertainments; one half for catering, the other for concerts and so on. The catering half was our Mess, the other half our Common Room. It was well lighted, there was a big open fire at each end behind guards. There were a lot of us, and most of us, being freed from family restraints, smoked liked chimneys. The air was blue with it. Cigarettes were cheap, probably still Players and Goldflake ten for three-pence and Woodbines five a penny. In the late twenties Players were five shillings a hundred.

This was a Depot, where we received new recruits, got them recorded and on to the conveyor belt for pay and rations, fitted them up with uniforms at the Q.M. stores, and then sent them off as required to various regiments to fill vacancies caused by non-combatant men being sent on active service. There was a blackboard on which each morning there would be a list of members 'on draft'—to Bracton, Rugeley, Catterick and other camps. They would have to go back to their billets, pack up their belongings, and go.

I was never on a draft, being given a job on the H.Q. staff in the Orderly Room, dealing with the Pay and Mess Book. 'Daily Orders' had to be sent up to the H.Q. Northern Command in York showing who had come on—or gone off—'the strength', with the appropriate Authority—AF/123/XYZ etc—and with relevant documents such as Last Pay Certificates. On these Daily Orders depended one getting a cheque to cover bed and board and pay packet. They had to be accurate.

The billets were only dormitories where we kept our suitcases. They were in houses which had been empty for years; damp showing on the walls, no heating. Dark-grey thin blankets on the beds which had to be folded up in neat piles each morning.

Each night after Roll Call at nine o'clock in the Arboretum, an officer or N.C.O. would call out the address of the billet and we would gather round, be checked from her list before being marched off to our repose. No sloping off to get a taste of Nottingham's night life!

Breakfast in the glass house was rather a chilly affair with cutlery, as I remember it, made of cast iron, heavy, cold, and squat in design. The midday meal was often salmon and rice rissoles. Tinned salmon, of course; provender I had never met with before—or since. With the U-boat menace at its height, rather surprising?

The very worst was on one occasion when I saw dried minced rabbit in wooden crates with no wrapping between it and the wood. Oh, cellophane, where wast thou?

The gutter press turned their attention to us. It was bad for recruiting, so something had to be done. Queen Mary took us over. We became Q.M.A.A.C. instead of W.A.A.C. New hat badges, not as neat as before. A small matter, but what was a very different one was that H.M. decreed that we must wear our uniforms two inches longer. I had no idea how to let a hem down. So I went out walking along the streets looking for a dressmaker, and, by good fortune, spotted a notice in a window. I asked if and when she could do it, and she said 'Come in, sit by the fire in your petticoat while I do it' and she wouldn't take anything for it. A pleasant memory; may her felicity ever increase.

About this time I nearly ran into disaster; nearly cooked my goose. They wanted volunteers for France. A certain cachet attached to the Overseas people, and I didn't feel I could miss it, so I volunteered. The officer sent for me. 'For Overseas service we need a birth certificate. Yours shows you are under age. We could discharge you immediately but as your work and conduct have been satisfactory we have decided against it, but if you put a foot wrong, out you go.' Phew!

To digress to the present:- I see in The Times that we are now the W.R.A.C., Women's Royal Army Corps. A good name. And that a Brigadier Anne Field is Controller Commandant.

My Army number would have been in four figures if someone had not carelessly misspelt my name necessitating a correction which put me much later at 14886. Bitter!

P.S. I think this rigmarole must stop here. I was demobbed when I was nineteen, nearer twenty, and I felt my life was over. And so in a sense it was—certainly youth.

Everybody had been keyed up and united in the national effort, and suddenly when the tension was snapped, we were tumbled into civilian life with the prosaic task of earning a living.

At twenty-five I had the ridiculous desire to write my autobiography, but certainly no leisure to spend on it, and I couldn't find a title—'Dear Dead days', or 'I'm a stranger here myself'. This little effort will have to do instead.

15/3/85

Dear Pamela,

Thank you very much for your charming postcard. It was very nice to hear from you.

I would send you more stories if I had them, but the vein is all but worked out. I might scrape the very bottom and get up the last remnants and send them along, but it will take time. Meanwhile I enclose an 'antique' document. One of our Daily Orders. I meant to include this with the account of our Army life, as a mark of authenticity, but it was not in the place where I fully expected it to be, and I concluded I had thrown it away in one of my tidying up drives. I felt shocked with myself for having done so after having had the sense to save a couple of copies all those years ago. It was a self-inflicted wound, very small of course, but sore enough. And then I accidentally came across them, in a very safe place. If you misplace this one, it doesn't matter, as I have another.

I remember the day when a young officer came into the office followed by an orderly bearing a typewriter which she placed on my desk. The officer said 'Oh, Prothero, we will have the Daily Orders typed in future.' 'But Ma'am, I have never used a typewriter.' 'Well, you've got all evening.' They were done and put in the signing tray, and I heard no more of them, so they must have been reasonably satisfactory.

I find this a little hard to believe now. But we were like that then. Have a go at anything. All pioneers and improvisers. Country girls went to the munitions factory in Hereford and were soon useful engineers, earning £1 a week, if you can believe it. It will be the ruin of them. They'll never be satisfied with sensible wages again!

What a giddy world it is?

I am at the end of the paper, so will conclude.

22/3/85

Dear Pamela,

Here, as requested, are the scrapings from the very bottom of the barrel. I would write if I had anything to write about. It would be a pleasure, but I have run out of material.

I did however come across an unexpected bit of advice the other day as to how to conduct oneself if suddenly confronted by a ghost—from Lewis Carroll—which I think you should know!

'When encountering a ghost for the first time it is necessary to remain as calm as may be and to retain the normal courtesies of civilised society, viz. on meeting a ghost in the street after dark a gentleman should <u>always</u> raise his hat.'

They don't write like that these days!

No Fourth Leaders in The Times any longer, all argy-bargy.

Summer visit to Tisbury won't be so long now with Easter nearly here.

Love

Taffy

P.S. Ghosts held a place in our minds, but not so witches; I never remember hearing of one. We did however have 'conjurors', but their role was entirely benevolent; with their special gift they could heal farm animals without even going to see them.

We knew one conjuror, my maternal uncle Evan Meredith of Llandeilo Graban. He said that the secret had been passed to him as a young man. When he told his father, a strict Baptist, he met with strong disapproval and was told to have nothing to do with it, to leave it entirely alone. But the young man thought 'I have been given this and I can do much good with it, I ought not just to let it lie idle.'

So the news got around that the mantle had fallen on him. Farmers came to see him. They would describe the symptoms of their ailing beast with particulars of any visible signs such as swellings or stiffness etc. The conjuror would listen attentively. The farmer would go back home and the beast would recover. There is mention of this in Howse's History of Radnorshire, a book which inexplicably I neglected to acquire when I could easily have done so. It is now quite unobtainable.

When I am on the subject of the somewhat unusual I will include two tales told to me as a child, for I believe they are genuine folklore and that something of the kind can be found in the folk tales of other lands. They were certainly handed down to me by word of mouth by people who had no truck with books. We pass from fact to fantasy.

The first was about a farmer who had the distressing experience of finding his animals dying suddenly with no sign of disease. A fine healthy young animal in the evening lying dead on the field next morning. Neither vet nor more experienced farmers could suggest a reason. It kept on happening. The farmer became desperately worried, seeing ruin for himself and his young family. What could it possibly be? No known cause. It came to him—there was only one thing—the Evil Eye. He knew there was a 'Wise Man' living a few miles away, so he went to see him. The 'Wise Man' said 'I'm afraid I cannot do very much for you. I can't call your enemy to book. I can only let you know who he is.' 'It is enough' said the farmer, 'I will see to the rest.'

'Well, when the next beast dies you must open him up and take out the heart. On a Sunday morning, when they are all in church and chapel, take the heart down to Nant wood and make a fire there with the dry sticks lying around. A small neat fire. It must be near the brook, within sound of running water. Let it get a firm hold and make a good deal of ash. Then lay on more sticks and place the heart on top. Before it is consumed your enemy will stand before you.'

The farmer did as he was told.

That Sunday morning they were in chapel as usual and all going on quietly and decently when the congregation was suddenly distracted by the behaviour of one old woman, an old lady who lived alone whom everyone knew and who was there every Sunday morning. She seemed to have got the fidgets and couldn't sit still. 'She must have been somewhere and picked something up!' But it got worse. 'She must be infested!' And then—unheard-of thing—she got up and walked out. We know where she went. But unfortunately, or perhaps fortunately, we don't know what happened, for the story ended there.

The other is about an afternoon service in the Disserth Church, one of the oldest churches in the County, with the original box pews in solid oak. You raised the latch on a string, opened the door, and when your family were all inside, you closed the door and dropped the latch, and you were in a little home from home.

This Sunday was in high summer in July, and a very close hot day. Too hot to last. It became very close and sultry. There would surely be a storm. They left the church door wide open to try to get a little air.

There was a very old clergyman there at the time, a truly venerable figure with white hair and long white beard. He had been there since his youth, and was genuinely revered and loved by all. The service proceeded as usual, and he made his way to the pulpit to preach the sermon. He was just beginning to give out the text when there was a vivid flash of lightning which seemed to fill the whole church and at the same time a very loud clap of thunder directly overhead, and also a heavy crunching sound on the gravel drive outside; and in through the open door there came a raving mad bull with bloodshot eyes and clouds of breath coming out of his nostrils which made his way up the aisle.

The clergyman knelt down and said 'Brethren, let us pray', and he proceeded to do so, aloud. The congregation of course followed suit and took to their knees, peering through the lattice work of their fingers at the bull, which seemed gradually to get less furious. Also in time it got smaller, and this went on until in time it was only a nice little bull calf. From then on it went through several metamorphoses, more than I can remember, but getting smaller all the time; sheep, hare, rabbit, mouse, etc, and in the end, a moth. Then it gave up and cried out with a loud voice and said 'Oh holy man, thou hast overcome me. Name thy punishment and let me be gone.'

'Oh, Evil Spirit, a heavy punishment must surely be thine for desecrating this sacred place. But it is not for me to mete out punishment. I shall continue to pray that we be protected against thy presence here.'

'Your prayer is answered. I, of my own volition, will take a vow not to come near for a period of nine hundred and ninety-nine years. But you must bury me deep down; not under earth and stone because for me they are but a flimsy covering. It must be in deep water.'

A man in the congregation got up out of his pew and came up the aisle, took out his snuff-box, emptied it, dusted it out thoroughly with his handkerchief and held it open. The moth hopped in. The man snapped the lid to. Then they went to the blacksmith to get the rim of the box soldered and a little ring and chain fixed, the other end fastened to a weight.

Somebody meanwhile had gone and got a pony and brought it up to the church porch. They lifted the old clergyman into the saddle; a man took hold of the bridle and led the horse along the winding path up the hillside and everyone followed. The hill, and all the hills around, wearing a chastened look after the storm and still steaming a little from the heavy downpour and hot earth.

After a while they reached the top and made their way to the Mawnpool. The strongest man in the parish went to the water's edge. They handed him the snuff-box and weight and he, with all his might, flung it into the centre of the pool. It sank, and the air bubbles came up, and kept on coming up. People looked at each other and said 'How very deep that pool must be.'

Any child on hearing this story would ask one question:- 'When will the nine hundred and ninety-nine years be up?'

And the answer they got:- 'Well, certainly not in <u>my</u> time. But in <u>yours</u>? Well, I couldn't be sure about that.'

12/7/85

Dear Pamela,

Elizabeth said on Sunday morning that you had had a most successful exhibition in London and that the cardigans went like hot cakes. Wait till the Newmarket folk see the jockey!

I have been thinking if there are any bits of my pre-war background that might possibly be of interest, since you have requested it.

I wonder if you would care to accompany me on my first day at school? I can't say the village school for there scarcely was a village and the school wasn't in it, but standing on its own roughly in the centre of our long straggling parish.

I knew that the event was in the pipeline. It had been put off for as long as possible as my parents felt the mile-and-a-half walk was a bit much. So I was six years old instead of the usual five.

The day came. I realised I was the centre of interest. One of my sisters (not the Harrogate one) put on a best hat and summer jacket, took a neat packet in hand containing, wrapped in a white dinner napkin, a bottle of cream for the Headmaster's wife. So we set off. How bright the sunshine on that eventful summer morning, how brand new the world!

Arriving at the school, we did not go in at the usual entrance but through the little private gate to the school house, along a little blue-chipped path. The Master's tiny kitchen garden on the left, the vegetables in little rows as straight as rulers, not a weed to be seen. On the right, a flower bed a yard wide, flanked by six-inch borders of neatly trimmed grass, with a little blue-chipped step-way through to the playground.

Mrs Williams and my sister exchanged pleasantries, and then I was handed over to the assistant teacher who took me to a small desk and gave me a book to read. I made no fuss.

My one idea was to escape notice, being an extremely shy child. And no wonder—I can hardly have seen another child of my own age. I certainly cannot remember one coming to our house.

So I applied myself quietly to my book—'The cat sat on the mat', and a picture of a quiet greyish-green tabby very similar to one of ours at home. I had no difficulty in reading it, as my family must have put in a lot of spade work on the simplest words. I seem to remember my mother saying that I could write my name and say the Lord's Prayer, which perhaps were then regarded as basic attainments before being passed on to other folk to be educated.

My sister only came once. I tagged along with two or three big girls from other farms who must have come a little out of their way to get me used to the route. No doubt arranged by our parents. But very soon I was going on my own and quite at home with it. Part of the way was over a common, with any number of peewits. They took no more notice of me than of the sheep, flying low down close over my head crying their long drawn-out 'pee-wit'. I seem to remember a kind of rubbing sound of their whirring wings, though I wonder what the ornithologists would say of this!

How fortunate in being able to walk to school instead of being transported! The famous St Teresa of Avila advised her nuns 'to take a spiritual exercise such as a country walk'. I had seven years of it, daily.

I was sorry to hear that you are having a lot of trouble with your health and very sorry that you have a lot of pain. I very much hope something can be done about it.

28/8/85

Dear Pamela,

In order to keep in touch with you I have cooked up a bit more about my schooldays of so long ago. What other topic shall we find when these come to an end?

I have been wondering how it was that no child ever came to our house before I went to school. Could we have been a bit unsociable? Then I was surprised I could have become so out of touch. Of course, it could not possibly have been otherwise. There were no motor cars. The farm houses were very scattered in such a thinly populated area, our friends often a couple or more miles or more away. A young child could not make the double journey. Prams or push chairs would have been of no use on our rough stony roads, not to mention when we went across fields and over stiles. Children all wore nailed boots, except when they were 'dressed up'. They were perfectly comfortable, were smooth with use, just right in frosty weather for sliding on any bit of ice we could find.

Had we no ponies and traps? We had, but nobody would have dreamt of using them for such a frivolous thing as going out to tea. Private Eye would have been on to it at once, and 'quite right too' everyone would have said. Life was harder then and poorer, but very sweet in parts.

So, we met other children for the first time in school. The day began with our sitting quietly in our places, each given a New Testament to learn two verses by heart. I enjoyed looking at the fire behind the guard. It had been lighted some time before we arrived and had burned clear and bright, and no ashes yet on the clean hearth. Very nice. The Master ended the half-hour with a moral talk, often trailing off into reminiscences, which was pleasant.

Then work began. How I admired those big thirteen-year-old boys! Boys? Men, surely, and more, statesmen. How grave and dignified their manner as they replaced the Testaments in the cupboard and brought out the lesson books. The general feel or atmosphere of our school was a bit like an old-fashioned church service, orderly, everything by rote, with no innovations and a touch of military neatness and precision.

So we set to; twice one are two and all that leads to. And history—ancient Britons and woad, Hengist and Horsa, Caractacus and our brave Edwalladour, the wicked Papists memorable from an illustration, a tall man, sinister face, long black cloak hiding a dagger no doubt. On to the Venerable Bede whom I venerated indeed. (Always a little intrigued with the Venerable Bede.) He was dictating the very last words of his book to a disciple. The candle, or it may have been a lamp, was just about to go out. Would it last until the last few words were written? It did. The young man looked up and said 'Master, it is finished.' The V.B. said 'My son, you speak truly. It is finished indeed.' And then he expired.

Mid-morning play-time came. We went out into the yard and often played rounders. The little vegetable garden and flower bed and blue-chipped path were now forbidden territory. It was hard to prevent the ball going over there. If it did, we were supposed to leave it there until the Master came out. But we couldn't wait. A boy would jump over, step daintily between the vegetables and hop back, hoping that the Master was in the back of the house and that he would not be caught. If he was, it meant the cane. It was the cane that kept the approach to the school-house neat and tidy.

The cane played a familiar part in our lives. It was kept in a table-drawer within arm's reach of the Master's sloping desk.

It didn't worry me on the whole. Usually one smart cut on one hand. One on both hands not very uncommon. I remember a boy getting two on both hands, which I didn't like. (A long wince I have had of it!)

There I think we must leave it for today.

I hope all goes to plan with you. More and more cardigans for Newmarket. It has been a cardigan year as far as the weather goes.

Take care.

10/10/85

Dear Pamela,

At twelve it was dinner time. ('Lunch' was a word that had not arrived with us. 'Luncheons' we had heard of, but they were not for the likes of us.)

The Master went into his house, and the assistant teacher to her nearby house. We went into the porch and got our schoolbags and brought them in and stood around the guard in front of the fire. We took out our medicine bottles, the old-fashioned sort with notches up the back, filled with milk in winter, cider in summer. Having had our drink, we ate whatever had been put up for us. It took about five minutes. Then we had till half-past-one at our disposal. On hot summer days we sometimes walked up a short distance to the bank of Boys. (A bank with us means a small hill. The 'Boys' comes from a tale of very long ago when two boys had a fright which ended in tragedy. I never heard the details. They had probably been lost with the passage of time, but the name stuck.)

This bank had grassy slopes and areas of fern (bracken) which grew very strong and tall, higher than our heads. We divided into two small groups. The 'hounds' turned their backs and counted up to a certain number to give us, the 'hares', a chance to run and hide in two's and three's, never singly, it would have been too frightening. When the hounds turned round they saw nothing but an expanse of fern. The hares must keep very still and quiet not to draw attention to ourselves. This was all very well unless the hounds came near. But who could wait there to be caught, killed and eaten! No, we tried to escape. The hounds now knew where we were, and came after us. We tried to run, but the fern was too dense. In the panic we would catch a foot on a strong stem and be sent headlong. The hounds fared no better, and it generally ended up with a heap of lost, breathless, slightly bruised children, with who was hare and who was hound forgotten.

It was a good game, and I am not the only one who remembered it, for many years later my elderly bachelor brother was sitting by his kitchen fire one morning after breakfast, looking out of the window when a car drew up, and out stepped an elegant lady, stylishly dressed and with the pleasantly confident air of one who is accustomed to being appreciated.

What has fallen to my lot this morning? he wondered. She came on, knocked, put her head round the door, greeted him, told him who she was, as he wouldn't have a chance to recognise the schoolgirl of years ago.

No, she wouldn't come in, but she felt she couldn't go by without looking him up, quite by chance that she was in the district and she didn't know at all when she would be again. Enquiries and local news followed, and she asked about me. 'Remember me to her when you write' she said 'and tell her I often think of the times we played hares and hounds.'

Sometimes we would go to the Shop, a mile and a half further down the lane to where it crossed the main road. Here we turned left along the main road and were soon in the metropolis, the Hundred House. A strange name for which I never heard an explanation. According to my atlas it is the only one in the world. 'Hundred House, Wales, United Kingdom' it says. It is a wonder to me that it got in, for it comprised only a Post Office, a shop, a pub, a vicarage and a boot shop, and, a little further away, a mill and two cottages. But it was a centre for a rural district before the motor car came in.

It was always a little thrill to go into the Shop. You turned the brass knob, opened the door, and the bell gave a little tinkle. Opposite was a sash window and in the sill 7lb jars of sweets. Mrs Williams, and what a nice kind woman she was, would weigh out the pennyworth of your choice into the little white, pointed bag, as much as you get for 10p now I suppose. There was tobacco, cigarettes and twist and chocolate too. On the counter a pile of the Brecon and Radnor.

On the left was the grocery counter, on the right drapery and gents' outfitters; corduroy trousers, shirts, underwear, dog collars for the clergyman. You could get a suit of clothes by bespeaking it, but that took a few days.

I don't remember much about the women's section, but certainly they did not aspire to 'fashions'. The children's part escapes my memory too, except for celluloid Eton collars, so easily kept clean, just a wipe with a soapy cloth. Boys wore neat knickerbockers of a dark shade, fastened by a neat band at the knee, and Norfolk jackets, with which an Eton collar went very well.

Further to the right was the Post Office counter and behind that the door into the Shop House. But to list all that they had is impossible. They tried to stock everything that was needed. The ceiling had stout metal hooks for holding lanterns, galvanised buckets, small farm tools, coils of ropes and balls of string, not an inch to spare anywhere. On the floor, brooms and besoms, forks and spades etc.

One thing in particular they must never be without, glass chimneys for our paraffin lamps. There was no gas or electricity of course. These glass chimneys had to stand the heat of the flame from the wick. Sometimes one would last for months and months, and then it would crack and be followed by a succession which would last no time at all. If you were without a chimney, it meant candlelight, which was dismal indeed.

Shopping done, we would trail back uphill to school, always arriving before half-past-one, though we had no watchers.

But there were days, and many of them, when it was too wet to go outside and we had to amuse ourselves in the schoolroom. When the noise we made grew intolerable for the Master in his house the other side of the porch, he came to deal with us. At his appearance, silence reigned. If he caught us playing a game we sometimes indulged in, chasing each other over the tops of the desks, the cane came into action. The lot of a village schoolmaster in those days was not a very rich one. Our Master was ready to help during the summer holidays on any farm where they were shorthanded in order to augment his slender salary which depended in some degree of the number of scholarships won during the year (Tell it not to the N.U.T., publish it not in the media!)

At four o'clock school was over and I set off for home. Unless I was 'kept in' for some misdemeanour. Then I was set to learn pieces of poetry by heart, chiefly Shakespeare:-

'This above all. To thine own self be true. And it must follow as the night the day, thou canst not then be false to any man.'

And Wolsey. 'Ambition! By that sin fell the angels. How can man then hope to profit by it? And when he thinks, poor man, full surely his greatness is a-ripening, then comes a frost, a killing frost, and then he falls as I do. If I had served my God as I have served my king He would not have thrown me over in my grey hairs.'

Not word perfect perhaps, but the gist I think. I had to stay in until the Master let me go.

When we came out of school, a few of us would go together for a short distance and then our ways would separate. When it came to the common, I had the world to myself; gorse bushes, poor white-ish grass a few inches high blowing in the wind, useless stuff which no animal would graze. 'Feg' we called it. On a cold evening under a grey sky it was something I like to remember. I would look out a gorse bush standing quite by itself. I had newspaper in my bag and a box of matches. I shoved the paper in the bottom of the bush, struck a match, and in no time had a fine blaze. I waited until it was burnt out and then went on my way warmed and cheered.

On exceptionally wet days I had another little diversion. Where I came down off the common there was a stream, too large to be called a brook, too small for a river. I crossed it by a footbridge below a little waterfall, and then the road ran alongside the water for a few yards. Normally the water came over the fall in little white cascades, but today the case was altered; it came over in one solid volume, the colour of milky tea, and the road and the river were one, too deep for short legs. But I knew what to do. I went up to the farmhouse, knocked on their back door and said 'Please may I go through your back kitchen? The flood is out.' So I dripped my way through, crossed their field and rejoined the lane further along my way.

Life was harder in many ways before the First World War, but we had one luxury that the moderns have not got; open fires in plenty. Coal was cheap. It came up from South Wales by rail, a ton was tipped out on the yard at Builth Station, and when we took our cart in, a casual labourer would shovel it up onto the cart, perhaps four feet up, for the charge of one shilling. This was very wrong. Nemesis has followed. Coal is now nearly too dear to buy, they have to try to make do with wood, casual labourers have disappeared, and so has the railway.

But when coal was plentiful, big glowing fires were a fact of life. There was no other heating for warmth, water or cooking. They were there from crack of dawn till bedtime, bright, cheerful, friendly focal points.

On the very hottest summer days we were bound to let the fire out after dinner, and so had to start a little one with wood chippings to boil water for tea-making.

Another advantage we had was that we were not slaves of the clock face. We had no time limits, but worked until the job was done in an unworried, unhurried way. There was one exception to this; the rare occasion when father felt he must have a day in London, which necessitated his catching the early morning train at Builth Road Junction, a walk of about seven miles. He had to be up and off at the crack of dawn. Mother had the gift of deciding when she would wake up and was never known to fail, but father couldn't trust to this and wasted the best part of a box of matches striking a light to see the time. When he finally set off we all heaved a sigh of relief.

At Builth Road the great Swansea-Newcastle Express would come thundering in, splendid in clouds of steam and general clangour. It could hardly be held back while the passengers got in. On the last carriage there was a small

47

white notice about two inches wide and just long enough for 'Euston' to be printed in black letters.

Father stayed one night at the Cora Hotel, which is near Euston Station, for a charge of five shillings, and it must have been without booking, for I never remember any letter being sent off. We who were left behind felt rather superior, and none the less so for no word being spoken about this frivolous episode.

It was the little Cambrian Railway that we lost, which ran through the Low Level Station at Builth Road in a westerly direction. The Express went through the High Level to the North East. The Cambrian Railway belonged to the age of innocence. It had a very high step to get in, which children could only manage with difficulty. The seats, six aside, no corridor, were well upholstered, and below the luggage grid on both sides were photographs of places of interest. We sat up straight and minded our manners. Old-fashioned country people felt they must have all clean underwear when they undertook a journey, 'in case of accident'.

The Cambrian ran through some of the loveliest scenery in Wales, through the Elan Valley close by the water's edge of the reservoirs. The little stations were a joy, competing which should be the best maintained and have the brightest flower beds. The Station Master and porter bustled with importance when a rain came in. Apart from the ordinary business, there might be a friend or relative abroad and a chance for a brief chat.

In those days it was not only the small rural station staff that took a pride and pleasure in their job. I remember hearing that at Stafford when the boat train from Euston to Holyhead drew in, the Station Master was on the platform dressed in a frock coat and silk top hat.

In the days before the motor car, the trains were our only link with the larger outside world, and the eyes of the younger generation were turned in that direction. Even now, I cannot think how they could manage without them. But they are much reduced. The last time I was at Builth Road, a poor, paltry two-carriage affair came slowly in. You wondered if it could make it, and when it did, whether it would start again. But far, very far, be it from me to disparage it, for it performs a vital purpose. And it was only saved by a whisker. I read somewhere that when Mr Wilson and his colleagues were discussing the closure of the railways, ours came up for consideration. It was losing money and it must go. George Thomas, who was then Secretary for Wales, was present but had taken no part in the discussions. When it was all settled, he said 'Ah well, I suppose there is no help for it. A pity though. The line runs through six marginal constituencies.'

2/12/85

Dear Pamela,

Walking was a way of life before motor cars became general. We walked as naturally as we breathed, and how pleasant it was, no traffic to beware of, no other pedestrians to avoid bumping into—the world to ourselves.

The walk over the hill to Builth was particularly good; described by the older generation as 'lightsome', a word I have not heard for over seventy years, but very descriptive I think. The springy turf under foot, and, as you got up higher, widening views of the surrounding countryside. When we came in sight of Builth we looked down on the Wye valley, and sometimes the little Cambrian train running alongside the river trailing small puffs of white steam, very pleasurable and exciting to a child.

Even the walks of a couple of miles or so when we went out to tea; a chance to build up anticipation, and on the return journey on a warm summer evening or a crisp autumn frost, to go over everything we had heard or seen. Country walking adds an indefinable, unconscious but very real quality to such rumination.

I could compare life without peaceful country walks to a printed page without margins.

In Builth at the turn of the century and for a few years afterwards the sale of farm stock took place in the High Street, which had obvious disadvantages and could occasionally be rather alarming when a bullock, bewildered by the strange surroundings, felt an urge to get away from it all and was prepared to use his horns to clear a path. You looked around for a shop door to get in out of his way. But usually the poor creatures were quiet and docile enough while the long, hard bargaining went on. Bargaining was a way of life to, not only for farm stock but for the purchases in the shops:-

'How much did you say it was?'

'Three and eleven three.'

'Yes, but how much to <u>me</u>?'

And so it went on, the customary thing, but embarrassing to the younger, spiritless generation. Three and eleven three then instead of 4/-. Now it's '99' or '95' instead of a pound. A very persistent piece of nonsense, and not very flattering to the supposed intelligence of the shopping public.

But before long a Smithfield was set up away from the shops and with proper pens and auctioneers—a great improvement. But they took to calling the bullocks 'steers', an American and meaningless word but enthusiastically adopted.

On a fine summer morning, under a blue sky and with almost dazzling sunshine, mother and I were walking up the High Street when she met a man who she appeared to know very well. She said to me 'This is your Uncle Tom'. I looked up and saw a man with white hair inclined to be curly, a round red face very sunburnt, and the merriest laughing blue eyes. He said 'Let me have her, let me take her back, I'll nurse her.' (He meant 'bring me up', not just take me on his knee.) Mother said something about questions being asked when she returned. I gazed at him with deep admiration. Mother bent down and said to me 'haven't you anything to say to your Uncle?' Interrupted in my contemplation and even then being awkward and never able to find words at the right time, all I could come out with was 'He'll do.'

These fairs and markets were a morning to afternoon affair, so something had to be found in the way of food at midday. Never a proper dinner, no meat, but just a bait to carry you on till you got home again. The men went into pubs to drink, but never to eat, not even bread and cheese I believe. Of course, no woman would dream of putting her foot inside one.

No, it was Hamer's Tea Shop on the first floor over their very good grocery shop. Hamer's Sixpenny Teas—bread and butter (jam? I'm not sure) ad lib and good quality. The days of shoddy stuff all advertisement and packaging were still far away. Hamer's also did small pastries and cakes à la carte which were my fancy and a permitted, but rare, indulgence.

Then when all the business was done, it was back to Grae House to get the trap out, on the days when we hadn't walked. What a job it was if we were towards the far end of two or three hundred traps with the backs right over the shafts. The ostler would come out and help, a poor man with one leg and an iron stump, but always cheerful. How could it be in those days when medical science was far less advanced than now? He would help to pull them all away until we could edge ours out. Then the ride home along the main road, often with the diversion of watching a farmer well known for his tipsy ways riding his pony a little way ahead of us. 'He'll be over. He's gone too far this time. He'll be in the ditch.' But no, his good pony would give a powerful hitch (or shift) and set him in an upright position, for the time being. Drunkenness has now largely disappeared, thank goodness.

Some Other Books from Logaston Press

A History of Presteigne

by Keith Parker. 256pp with many photographs, maps and illustrations. Paperback £9.95. ISBN 1 873827 79 2

Having lived and taught in Presteigne for many years, Keith Parker has gradually accumulated a wealth of information with which he has written this detailed and lively account of the town's history. A dry account of civic meetings it is not, rather a story of a town always fighting for survival be it from plague, fire, or economic recession. Through the tribulations emerge the border spirit typified in Presteigne.

Walks in Southern Powys & the Borders

by Andrew Johnson, 112pp, line illustrations and maps.
£4.95 ISBN 0 9510242 8 0

This book includes 35 walks of two hours duration in an area roughly bounded by Llanidloes, Rhayader, Builth Wells, Brecon, Hay-on-Wye, Kington and Knighton.

Guide to the Castles of Radnorshire

by Paul Remfry. 160pp with some 35 photographs, plans and maps. £7.95 ISBN 1 873827 54 7

The history of the centuries of warfare and changing alliances in Radnorshire is covered in some detail for it provides the background to the construction of the castles; indeed, much of the recorded history is about the regular sieges and their capture. Detailed information is also given about all the castle sites.

Is it still raining in Aberfan? - A Pit and its People

By Melanie Doel and Martin Dunkerton, 160pp, over 100 black and white photographs. Large format paperback (260mm x 230mm). £9.95 ISBN 0 9510242 9 9

A record of the history and life of the Merthyr Vale Colliery and its people from its inception to its closure, in the words of miners, their families and others as well as in archive photographs and those taken by Martin Dunkerton from 1984 onwards.